my first SCIENCE BOOK

my first
SCIENCE
BOOK

explore the wonders of science
with this fun-filled guide:

- kitchen-sink chemistry
- fantastic physics
- backyard biology

Susan Akass

CICO kidz

To the children who have made teaching science fun

Published in 2015 by CICO Books
An imprint of Ryland Peters & Small Ltd
20–21 Jockey's Fields, London WC1R 4BW
341 E 116th St, New York, NY 10029

www.rylandpeters.com

10 9 8 7 6 5 4 3 2 1

Text © Susan Akass 2015
Design and photography © CICO Books 2015
Photographs on pages 9 and 109 © Corbis

A CIP catalog record for this book is available from the
Library of Congress and the British Library.

ISBN: 978 1 78249 254 2

Printed in China

Editor: Clare Sayer
Designer: Alison Fenton
Photographer: Penny Wincer
Illustrator: Hannah George
Stylist: Sophie Martell

In-house Editor: Anna Galkina
In-house designer: Fahema Khanam
Art director: Sally Powell
Head of production: Patricia Harrington
Publishing manager: Penny Craig
Publisher: Cindy Richards

Contents

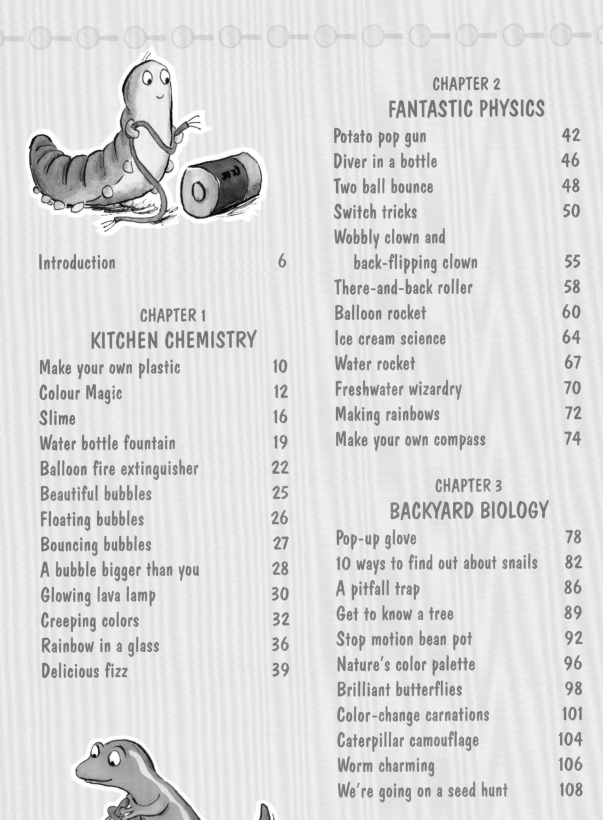

Introduction

Science is to do with finding out about the world and how it works, which is a big subject! You may have already started studying science at school, but this is not like a school science book. This science book is all about WOW projects that you can easily do at home without special equipment or dangerous chemicals. These are projects that will help you learn about the world, while having fun!

In this book we have divided the projects up into three chapters, each one looking at a different part of science.

In **Kitchen Chemistry**, with the help of some fizzes, bangs, pops, gooey stuff, and color changes, you can begin to discover the amazing science of chemistry and how-easy-to-find kitchen chemicals react with one another to make something new.

In **Fantastic Physics**, using balloon rockets, potato pop guns, rainbows, trick switches, and other fun projects, you can begin find out about the forces and energy that rule our world, what makes things stop and go, what causes change and how things work.

In **Backyard Biology** you will begin to explore the wonderful natural world that exists just outside your back door. You can learn about how amazing trees are, or how a snail sees. You can try your hand at worm charming or change the color of a flower.

There is just so much to explore in science! At the end of each project there is a short passage explaining why something fantastic has happened or giving you some more information. We hope you will use these as a starting point for exploring more science, but you could just get on with the projects, have lots of fun, and say "Wow, that was amazing!"

Science equipment

Most of the chemicals and equipment used in this book are things you can find in your kitchen or around your house. We have included a list of these things so that you can check whether you have them at home. If you haven't, ask if they can be put on the shopping list for your family's next visit to the supermarket! For a few of the projects, however, you may have to buy some special materials. Each project has a "You will need" list, so check you have everything on the list before you start.

Active dried yeast

Baking soda (bicarbonate of soda)

Balloons—some round and some long

Cans with plastic lids (like coffee cans or baby formula cans)

Citric acid

Coffee filters

Colored wool scraps

Confectioner's sugar (icing sugar)

Cooking oil

Cornstarch (cornflour)

Disposable plastic beakers

Double-sided sticky tape

Egg cartons

Elastic bands

Empty jam jars

Food coloring in lots of different colors

Glycerine

Large plastic bottles (2-quart/2-liter)

Modeling clay

Plastic bottle with sports cap (pop top)

Plastic drinking straws

Plastic wrap (cling film)

Sticky labels

Sticky tape

String

Sugar

Table tennis (ping pong) ball

Vinegar—white household vinegar is best for most projects

Liquid detergent—not antibacterial, and the thicker the better

Project levels

Level 1
Projects are simple, quick, and use materials you are likely to have around your house

Level 2
May be a little more difficult and may use some materials you need to buy specially

Level 3
May need special materials and usually need some help from an adult

chapter 1
Kitchen Chemistry

Make your own plastic

Look around you and you will discover that a huge number of the things you own and use are made of plastic. You may or may not know that all these plastics are made from oil—the same oil that gasoline (petrol) is made from. Don't worry, we're not using gasoline to make plastic today, we're going to use milk. That's right—milk!

You will need:

....

1 cup (240 ml) whole milk

Measuring jug or small pan

1 tablespoon white vinegar

A strainer (sieve)

A bowl

A spoon

Paper towels

Cookie cutters or molds for play dough or sugarcraft

1 Ask an adult to help you to heat the milk in a microwave or in a pan on the stovetop. It needs to be hot, but not boiling. Make sure you wear an oven glove when handling the jug or pan.

2 Add the vinegar and stir. The milk will "curdle"—this is when solid pieces start to clump together, leaving a clear liquid. Leave it for a few minutes to cool so it is safe to work with.

3 Put the strainer over the bowl and pour the milk mixture into it. The solid pieces will be caught in the strainer. Wait for a little while for all the liquid to drain through, then tip the liquid down the sink as you don't need it.

4 Tip the solid white pieces from the strainer into the bowl and work them with the back of a spoon or with your fingers. Keep squishing them together until they become a smooth lump, a bit like a piece of play dough. This is your plastic.

The science
BEHIND THE MAGIC

The plastic you have made is a simple one called casein. When the curds in the milk react with the vinegar the casein is left in blobs. Casein is a long string molecule (see page 112) similar to the plastic molecules made from oil. As the casein dries it hardens because the molecules bond together more tightly.

5 Fold up some paper towels into a pad with several layers. Tip the plastic on top and leave it for about 30 minutes so that some of the water that is still in it is soaked up by the paper.

6 Now use your cutters to mold the plastic into different shapes. Leave the shapes to dry out and harden up for a couple of days—near a warm radiator is ideal. You can now paint or decorate your shapes—this is a great way to make Christmas decorations!

Make PLASTIC from MILK!

Color magic

This experiment makes science look like magic! Add a few drops of another liquid to your red cabbage water and watch it instantly change color! The indicator lets you know if a liquid is an acid, an alkali, or in between (neutral). Strong acids are very dangerous but you will find weak ones that are safe to handle—like lemon juice and vinegar—in your kitchen. Acids give foods a sour or "sharp" taste. Alkalis are substances that react with acids and neutralize them. Soap and detergent are alkaline.

You will need:

½ red cabbage

Kitchen scissors

A medium-sized bowl

A packet of about 10 small transparent plastic cups

A strainer (sieve)

A pitcher (jug)

Lots of different liquids from your kitchen such as lemon juice, white wine vinegar, liquid detergent, apple juice, lemonade, baking soda (bicarbonate of soda) (mixed with a little water). Colorless or light-colored liquids are best

Yoghurt pots or small cups

A medicine dropper (you could use a teaspoon but a dropper is more fun!)

Sticky labels

A pencil

SAFETY FIRST

Ask an adult before using any liquids, especially cleaning liquids.

1 Pull the layers of the cabbage apart and use the scissors to cut the leaves into small pieces. You don't need the thick stems. Put the pieces into the bowl.

2 Ask an adult to help you boil a kettle and then cover the cabbage with boiling water and leave for about 10 minutes.

3 While the mixture is cooling, line up the plastic cups on a table or work surface and assemble all the different liquids you are going to test. Make sure you ask an adult which ones you can use and be especially careful with any cleaning products—do not use these without an adult's help.

4 When the cabbage mixture is cool pour it through the strainer (sieve) into the pitcher (jug). The liquid is your indicator—it should be a nice purple color (you can throw away the cooked cabbage).

5 Pour a little cabbage water into each cup so there is about ½ inch (1 cm) of liquid in each cup.

6 Cut a lemon in half and squeeze the juice into a yogurt pot (or use lemon juice from a bottle). Use the dropper to add a few drops of lemon juice to one cup. What color does it turn? Label the cup *"Lemon juice"* and remember that lemon juice is an **acid**. Wash the dropper—you will need to wash the dropper each time you use it so that you don't mix up the different liquids.

7 Ask an adult to dissolve a little liquid detergent in some warm water in another pot. (This can hurt your skin so you shouldn't touch it.) With the adult's help, add a few drops of the liquid to the next cup. What color does it turn? Label the cup *"Liquid detergent"*. Remember that dishwasher detergent dissolved in water makes a strong **alkali**.

8 Now pour a little vinegar into another yogurt pot and add a few drops to the next cup. Continue to add different liquids to the cups. Be a good scientist and label each one as you go. You should end up with a range of different color liquids in the cups. Some liquids won't have changed the color of the cabbage water. These liquids are **neutral**—neither acid nor alkali.

COLOR-change CABBAGE!

9 Now arrange all the cups on the work surface. Put the acids at one end—these are all shades of red (like the lemon juice). Put the alkalis at the other—these are shades of green and blue (like the dishwasher detergent). Put the neutral ones in the middle; these didn't change the color of the cabbage water. You can tell which are the strongest acids and alkalis by how dramatic the color change is! Put the strongest acid at one end, the strongest alkali at the other, and then try to decide in which order the others will go in order of how strong they are.

The science
BEHIND THE MAGIC

All liquids have something called a pH value, which tells you about their chemical makeup and how they react with other chemicals. The scale ranges from 0 to 14. A liquid with a pH value between 0 and 7 is acid. A pH value of around 7 is neutral and between 7 and 14 the liquid is an alkali. Acids with very a low pH or alkalis with a very high pH are very strong and very dangerous.

Slime

This is a chance to get very messy—perhaps it's better to leave this project until the summer, when you can do it outside! Cornstarch (cornflour) is wonderful stuff—just try this out to see how amazing it is.

You will need:

Large packet of cornstarch (cornflour)

Tablespoon

A large bowl

Measuring pitcher (jug)

Water—about 1 cup (240 ml)

A wooden spoon for mixing

Food coloring (optional)

1 Put 10 heaped tablespoons of cornstarch (cornflour) into a large mixing bowl.

2 Pour about a quarter of the water into the bowl and start stirring.

SQUELCH IT, squeeze it, SQUISH IT!

3 Keep adding water, a little at a time, until you have a thick paste. Don't add too much at once. If the mixture gets a bit too runny add some more cornstarch (cornflour).

4 Add two teaspoons of food coloring and mix it in well.

Tip

If you have enough cornstarch (cornflour), why not double or triple the quantities listed above so that you have plenty of slime for you and your friends to play with.

5 Slowly poke your fingers into the slime and stir them around. The slime will feel like a thick liquid, which will ooze between your fingers.

The science
BEHIND THE MAGIC

Imagine the cornstarch (cornflour) molecules (see page 112) as being like cubes, and the water molecules as being like much smaller spheres (balls). When you add the water to the cornstarch the big cubes can move around because they are spaced out, with the water molecules between them. The mixture is a liquid. But when you punch the mixture hard, the water molecules are squeezed inside the cornstarch molecules and the cubes become tightly packed together, like bricks, and can't move. This is now a solid. Let the pressure go, the water molecules pop back out and it's back to a liquid!

6 Now punch down hard on it. Surprise! It feels like a solid. Squeeze a handful hard to make a solid ball. Throw it from hand to hand or to someone else. Does it stay solid?

Water bottle fountain

This is an experiment that you should definitely do outside. Find a good flat surface to stand the bottle on and be warned: once you have set this up don't be tempted to go back to it—even if it hasn't gone off straightaway. When it goes it will go very suddenly, and if you are too close you will get showered with very smelly vinegar.

You will need:

Paper towel

A teaspoon

Baking soda (bicarbonate of soda)

A small water bottle with a sports cap (pop top)

White household vinegar (quite a lot!)

Funnel (optional)

1 Tear a piece of paper towel into quarters. Put 2 teaspoons of baking soda (bicarbonate of soda) onto one quarter and fold it up into a package.

2 Make sure the cap of the bottle is pushed down (in the closed position). Then unscrew the cap from the bottle and keep it to one side, ready to put back on.

3 Push the folded paper towel package into the bottle.

4 Working quickly, half-fill the bottle with vinegar. This is easier if you have a funnel but you can do it without.

5 Quickly screw the cap onto the bottle and give it a shake.

6 Stand the bottle upright and move back.

7 Wait for the fountain—it should only take a few moments for the reaction to happen!

The science
BEHIND THE MAGIC

The baking soda (bicarbonate of soda) reacts with the vinegar to produce a foam of carbon dioxide gas. This builds up the pressure inside the bottle until it is strong enough to force up the cap and shoot the foam into the air.

Balloon fire extinguisher

If you don't like balloons bursting this probably isn't the best project for you—but it's fun and interesting. Have you heard of the fire triangle? The fire triangle tells you that you need three things for a fire to burn—fuel, heat, and oxygen. Take away any of those and the fire will go out. In this project you can try putting out a candle using three different balloon fire extinguishers, but you will need an adult's help for this.

You will need:

Balloon pump

3 similar-sized balloons but in different colors, ideally white, blue, and yellow

A teaspoon

Baking soda (bicarbonate of soda)

Small plastic bottle—the balloon neck must be able to fit over the top of the bottle.

Funnel

A tablespoon

White household vinegar

Water

Votive candle (tealight)

Second timer

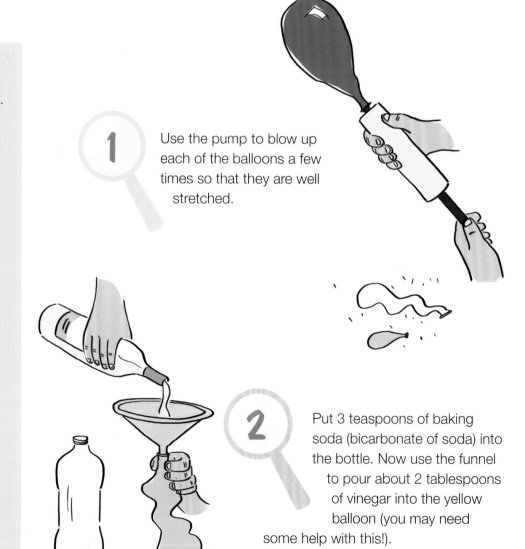

1 Use the pump to blow up each of the balloons a few times so that they are well stretched.

2 Put 3 teaspoons of baking soda (bicarbonate of soda) into the bottle. Now use the funnel to pour about 2 tablespoons of vinegar into the yellow balloon (you may need some help with this!).

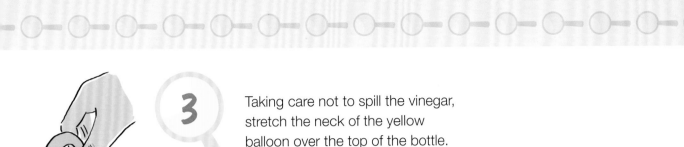

3 Taking care not to spill the vinegar, stretch the neck of the yellow balloon over the top of the bottle.

4 Now hold the balloon up so that the vinegar spills into the bottle. The vinegar and baking soda (bicarbonate of soda) will react to produce a foam of carbon dioxide gas, which will inflate the balloon. If it doesn't inflate that much, twist the neck of the balloon so no carbon dioxide escapes (you'll need a helper at this point), add some more baking soda (bicarbonate of soda) and vinegar to the bottle, and then reattach the balloon. When it is well inflated tie a knot in the neck.

5 Now blow up the white balloon, using the pump, until it is about the same size as the yellow balloon and tie a knot in the neck.

6 Wash out the funnel and use it to pour some water into the blue balloon. Now use the pump to blow it up until it is the same size as the white and yellow ones. You now have three balloon fire extinguishers — which do you think will put out a fire?

7 You will need an adult's help for the testing stage. Ask an adult to light a votive candle (tealight). If you are feeling brave, hold the white, air-filled balloon just above the candle (NOT in the flame) for just 15 seconds or until the balloon bursts—whichever is quicker. You may want to ask an adult to do this while you cover your ears! What happens to the balloon and the flame?

8 Next try with the blue, water-filled balloon. Hold it above the flame for just 15 seconds, no longer, or until it bursts—whichever is quicker. What happens to the balloon and flame?

9 Finally use the yellow carbon dioxide filled balloon for just 15 seconds or until it bursts. What happens to the balloon and flame this time? Which was the best fire extinguisher?

The science
BEHIND THE MAGIC

The air from the white balloon does not put out the flame because it just gives it more oxygen. The blue balloon won't have burst at all—the water takes away the heat from the candle so the rubber doesn't melt and burst. The yellow balloon extinguishes the flame because carbon dioxide gas is heavier than air so when the balloon bursts the gas sinks down over the flame and drives away all the oxygen. Many real fire extinguishers are filled with carbon dioxide for this reason—you will probably see them around your school, in restaurants, and other public places.

Which ONE will WORK?

Beautiful bubbles

Everyone loves to play with bubbles and the bigger the bubble the better. There are several different bubble projects to try here, but first make your very own super powerful bubble mixture and use it for a few fun investigations.

You will need:

Measuring pitcher (jug)

Water—distilled water makes the best bubbles—you can often buy this in pharmacies or in household stores (for using in irons)

Plastic pitcher (jug)

Washing detergent (not antibacterial)—thicker brands are better

A tablespoon (15 ml)

Glycerine—you can find this in the baking section of supermarkets

Drinking straws

Thin wire or wire coathanger

Large flat dish or saucer (plant pot holders are ideal)

1 Use the measuring pitcher (jug) to measure 7 fl oz (200 ml) of distilled water and pour it into the plastic pitcher (jug). Add 2 fl oz (50ml) of washing detergent. Use the tablespoon to measure exactly 15 ml of glycerine and add it to the jug. Stir everything together and then leave it and be patient. The mixture makes the best bubbles if you leave it for at least one day before you use it.

2 Make bubble blowers out of straws or twist wire into different shapes to make wands. Pour the bubble mixture into a large flat dish or saucer big enough to fit your big bubble blowers. Does a square bubble wand make a square bubble? What is the biggest bubble you can make? Watch how the liquid swirls around the bubble and makes beautiful colors.

BLOW them, POP them, see them FLY!

Floating bubbles

Bubbles will fly away in the wind but in the end they will either pop or fall back to earth, where they will pop when they touch the ground. Well, not always. Look what happens to the bubbles in this project.

You will need:

A tablespoon

White household vinegar

Large clear bowl

Baking soda (bicarbonate of soda)

Bubble mixture and wand (see page 25)

1 Pour 2 tablespoons (30 ml) of vinegar into the bowl and add 1 tablespoon (15 ml) of baking soda (bicarbonate of soda).

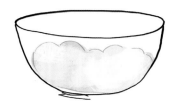

2 Watch as the two ingredients react together and foam up in the bowl.

The science
BEHIND THE MAGIC

As you have already seen (see page 22), when you mix vinegar and baking soda (bicarbonate of soda) together they produce the gas carbon dioxide. Carbon dioxide is heavier than air so it stays at the bottom of the bowl. When you blow bubbles into the bowl they start to drop down—this is because of gravity. However, the air inside the bubbles is lighter than the carbon dioxide, so the bubbles float on it—a bit like a duck on water! This is why the bubbles appear to hover.

3 When the reaction has died down, blow some bubbles into the bowl. Watch the bubbles hover in the air—why aren't they dropping down?!

Bouncing bubbles

Have you ever tried to catch a bubble? The chances are that as soon as you touched one it popped. Here is a clever way of catching a bubble and seeing it bounce. You could even play bubble tennis, bouncing it to a friend.

You will need:

Knitted gloves

Bubble mixture and wand
(see page 25)

1 Put a knitted glove on one hand. Blow a few bubbles and hold out your gloved hand to catch one. It won't pop, it will bounce.

2 Bounce it on to a friend or bounce it from hand to hand. How many pats can you give it before it bursts?

The science
BEHIND THE MAGIC

Grease is the enemy of bubbles. Soap molecules are attracted to grease and so when a bubble touches some grease the soap molecules are pulled away from the soap film and the bubble pops. Our hands are slightly greasy so if a bubble touches a hand it pops. Gloves stop the bubble touching the grease. Bubbles also pop when water evaporates from them. The glycerine in the bubble mix slows down evaporation so the bubbles last longer for your tennis game.

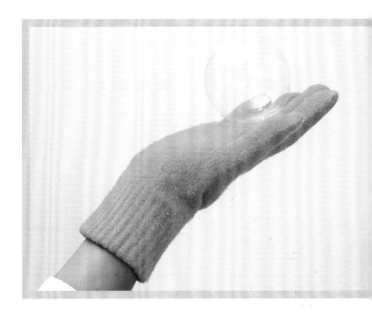

Play bubble TENNIS!

A bubble bigger than you

Imagine being inside a bubble! Can you really make a bubble that's big enough—a bubble bigger than you? You will need a lot of bubble mix but it's the same recipe as before, just made with a lot more of each ingredient! It's easy to make and a fun idea for a party.

You will need:

....

2 clean buckets

Measuring pitcher (jug)

20 pints (10 liters) water (see Tip)

1 cup (250 ml) washing detergent (not antibacterial) —thicker brands are better

2 tablespoons glycerine

A tablespoon

A large mixing spoon

A small wading pool (paddling pool)

A hula hoop that you can step through—clean it well before you use it

1 A couple of days before you need it, make up the bubble mix. Make it in two buckets so the buckets are not too full and heavy—each bucket should contain 10 pints (5 liters) of water, ½ cup (125 ml) washing detergent, and 1 tablespoon of glycerine. Mix well and leave the buckets in a safe place where they won't get knocked over. Cover the tops to keep the mixture clean.

2 On the day of the party or whenever you are ready to use it, very slowly pour the mixture from the buckets into the wading pool (paddling pool), trying not to let the surface get foamy.

See the WORLD through a BUBBLE

Tip

Bubble mixes can vary from place to place because of the differences in the water. Soft water is best for bubbles. If you live in a place with very hard water, where you get lots of chalky limescale building up in your kettle or around your faucets (taps), you would be better off using distilled water, which you can buy at the grocery store or from gas (petrol) stations.

3 Now for the bubble making—ask an adult to help you. Place the clean hoop flat in the pool so it is covered in the bubble mixture. Stand in the middle of the hoop and get the adult to pull the hoop straight up around you as quickly as possible. Look out through the bubble and see the world in a whole new way! How long does the bubble last?

4 Try experimenting on your own too: Lift the hoop vertically out of the mixture with a film across it and let the wind blow monster bubbles.

Glowing lava lamp

You'll soon be hypnotized watching the bubbles rise through the oil in this beautiful lava lamp. If you make your lamp after dark, drop in a glow stick, switch off the lights, and you will have an even more magical experience.

1 Before you start making your lava lamp, have a bit of fun investigating oil and water. Fill a glass with water and then drop in a teaspoon of oil. Watch what happens to the oil. Stir it hard to mix it into the water and then wait and watch!

You will need:
....

A glass tumbler

Vegetable oil (you will need quite a lot)

A teaspoon

A funnel

Water

A clear plastic bottle

Food coloring

Alka-Seltzer tablets (or fizzing Vitamin C tablets)

A glow stick (optional)

2 Now to make your lamp. Using the funnel, pour water into the bottle until it is about a quarter full.

3 Using the funnel again, pour in the vegetable oil until the bottle is a bit more than three-quarters full. You need to leave room for your glow stick.

4 Watch as the oil and water separate into two layers with the heavier water sitting at the bottom. Wait until the oil and water have settled.

LET yourself be MESMERIZED...

5 Add about 12 drops of food coloring. Watch as it falls through the oil—the coloring will not mix with the oil. It will fall until it meets the water and will then sit on top of the water for a few seconds before bursting into the water and then spreading out in the water. Gently twist the bottle a few times to help the color mix with the water, but don't stir or shake it.

6 Now, break an Alka-Seltzer (or fizzing Vitamin C) tablet into about 4 smaller pieces. Drop one piece of the tablet into the bottle. It will drop through the oil into the water and begin to fizz. Watch as bubbles begin to erupt through the oil. When the bubbling begins to slow down, add another piece of Alka-Seltzer and it will start all over again.

The science

BEHIND THE MAGIC

Oil and water don't mix and oil floats on top of water. This is because oil is less dense than water. When you drop the piece of Alka-Seltzer into the lava lamp bottle it drops through the oil and into the water. Here it begins to fizz, releasing small bubbles of carbon dioxide. These bubbles get attached to blobs of water and act like floats. The blobs rise up to the surface through the oil. When they reach the surface, the gas escapes and without its float to hold it up, the more dense water sinks back down.

7 For the full glow show, bend your glow stick to activate it, drop it into the bottle, and switch off the lights.

Creeping colors

What color is the ink in your black marker pen? Did you say black? Think again! Using filter paper, watch as water creeps through different inks and spreads them out into amazing strips of different colors. This is called chromatography and it lets you find out just what different colors make up the inks you use. Try this experiment using several glasses and pencils so you can work on lots of different color inks at the same time.

You will need:

Coffee filter papers (white ones, not unbleached brown ones)

Scissors

A glass or clear plastic cup

Sticky tape

A pencil

A pack of colored marker pens

1 Cut several long strips of coffee filter paper about ½ inch (1 cm) wide and just longer than the height of the glass.

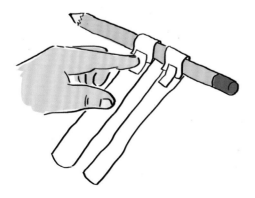

2 Tape each strip to the middle of a pencil. You can probably tape two, or even three, strips to each pencil if the strips are narrow and your glass quite wide.

3 Place the pencil over the top of the glass with the paper strips dangling down inside. Check that the ends hang just above the bottom of the glass.

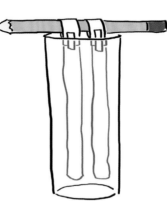

4 Take away the pencil while you pour enough water into the glass so that the bottom of the paper strips will just reach it.

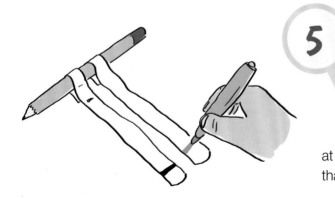

5 Using a different colored marker pen for each strip, draw a line across the bottom of each paper strip, about 1 inch (2.5 cm) from the bottom. Let it dry and then draw another line, using the same color, over the top of the first. Do this a couple of times so you have plenty of ink on your paper. In pencil, at the top of the strip, write what color you have used on that strip (it will be surprisingly difficult to tell later on).

How many COLORS make BLACK?

6 Place the pencil back over the glass. The ends of the strips should just hang in the water but the ink line must be above the water.

7 Wait and watch as the water creeps up the paper, carrying the ink with it and separating it out into different colors. Which color markers only have one color ink in them? Which are made up of lots of colors? Which has the most colors?

The science
BEHIND THE MAGIC

Some inks are made up of more than one color. The molecules of the chemicals that make these colors have different "likes." Some are attracted to water more than paper and some are attracted to paper more than water. The ones that are most attracted to water are carried along with it quickly as it travels up the paper. The ones that are attracted to paper stick to the paper and don't move much, if at all.

Rainbow in a glass

Normally, if you added water that has been colored with different food colorings to a glass, the colors would mix together. For example, if you mixed yellow and blue water you would get green. In this project you slowly add different colored waters to a glass and end up with a beautiful rainbow of different layers of color!

You will need:

4 plastic cups

A teaspoon

Sugar

A measuring pitcher (jug)

Hot water from the faucet (tap)

A spoon for mixing

Blue, red, green, and yellow food coloring

A glass tumbler

A plastic medicine syringe

1 Line up the four plastic cups and add sugar to them as follows:
Cup 1—1 teaspoon
Cup 2—2 teaspoons
Cup 3—3 teaspoons
Cup 4—4 teaspoons

2 Add 2 fl oz (60 ml) of hot water from the faucet (tap) to each of the cups and then stir each one until all the sugar has dissolved. (If the sugar won't dissolve ask an adult to help you to put the cups into the microwave, heat them for 30 seconds, and then stir again)

3 Add blue food coloring to cup 1, red to cup 2, green to cup 3, and yellow to cup 4. Stir each cup again. (Wash the spoon between stirs!)

4 Pour the yellow water into the glass tumbler.

The science
BEHIND THE MAGIC

When sugar is dissolved in water, the water becomes more dense. (Dense means heavier for the same amount of water.) The more sugar you add, the more dense the water will be. In the glass, the heavier (more dense) yellow water stays at the bottom and the less dense waters float in layers above it. The lightest (least dense) blue water floats on the top.

5 Fill the plastic syringe with green water. Hold the tip of the syringe just above the surface of the yellow water and, very slowly and carefully press the plunger so that the green water dribbles down over the yellow. You may have to fill the syringe several times depending on the size of your syringe. Do the same with the red water next, and finally the blue. The four different colors will stay in separate layers to make a rainbow!

MAKE a liquid RAINBOW!

Delicious fizz

Have you ever bitten into a sherbet lemon candy and felt a cold fizz on your tongue? The fizz and the coldness are chemistry happening in your mouth! Usually in science we say, "Never put anything in your mouth!" but this is an exception. It's a quick and very tasty project.

1 Mix together all the dry ingredients in the bowl.

You will need:

A small bowl or cup

A measuring spoon

A measuring cup

¼ cup (30 g) confectioner's (icing) sugar

½ teaspoon citric acid

½ teaspoon baking soda (bicarbonate of soda)

Spoon for mixing

2 Taste the mixture and feel what is happening! Enjoy!

The science
BEHIND THE MAGIC

Here you have an acid (citric acid) mixing with the base (baking soda)—a bit like other experiments (see page 21). While they are both dry they don't react. As soon as you put them in your mouth, saliva mixes with them and they begin to react and produce carbon dioxide—that's the fizz! The coldness is because this reaction takes heat from its surroundings—in this case, your tongue so it feels strangely, but nicely, cold. The sugar doesn't cause any reaction at all—it just tastes nice!

SCIENCE on your TONGUE!

chapter 2
Fantastic Physics

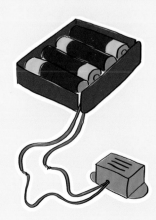

Potato pop gun

How about a bit of target practice? For this simple project your only ammunition will be a potato—or maybe two or three because you will find it's so much fun you will want to keep going. Just make sure that the potatoes you use are not needed for your dinner! This is another project you should definitely do in a big outside space, and, most importantly, NEVER fire your pop gun toward a person or animal.

You will need:

A length of copper pipe, about 24 inches (60 cm) long

A metal nail file

Colored chalks to draw a target

A few large potatoes

Water-soluble ink or paint and a small pot (optional)

A length of dowel (round wood) or garden cane that fits into the pipe and is about the same length as the pipe

1 You can buy copper pipe cut to length or ask an adult to help you saw a piece. Be careful that the pipe doesn't get bent or dented as you saw—the tube needs to be completely straight and smooth. Use the metal nail file to file away any rough edges from the ends.

2 Find a place to draw a target—maybe a fence or a tree. You need a good length of backyard— about 4 or 5 yards (meters) to fire along. Draw the target like an archery target with different rings for different scores, with the bullseye in the center scoring the highest number of points!

Who can SCORE a BULLSEYE?

3 Put the potato on a firm surface—the ground will do fine. Hold it still and push one end of the tube right through the potato. This will make a plug of potato in the tube. Make sure that the potato completely fills the end of the tube.

4 Turn the tube over and do the same with the other end so that both ends are plugged with potato.

5 If you want your potato to make a mark when it hits the target, pour a little ink or paint into a pot and dip one end of the tube into it.

6 To fire your spud gun you need to poke the piece of dowel or garden cane into the other end of the tube. To do this in one go can be a bit tricky so first push the stick a little way into the tube, pushing the potato in by about ½ inch (1 cm) so that the stick can't slip sideways. Then rest the tube on a table or back of a chair so you can hold it steady. Make sure that there is no one in the way, take aim, and poke hard! The inky potato plug will shoot out with a pop—and maybe even a puff of smoke! It should make a splat of ink on the target (if you hit it).

7 Before you go again, clear the tube. Push out the piece of potato that is still in the tube by using your poking stick. It should come out with a pop. Load up with more potato and try again. How accurate can you get?

The science
BEHIND THE MAGIC

The pieces of potato jammed into each end of the pipe are so tight that no air can get in or out. When the potato at the back is pushed in with the dowel, the space between the two plugs of potato becomes smaller, squeezing the air inside which means the pressure builds up. In the end the pressure is so great that it forces the potato out of the front of the tube.

Diver in a bottle

All divers want to sink to the bottom of the ocean so that they can see the fish or explore old wrecks. You can send this pen cap diver to the bottom of the bottle just by squeezing the bottle. It floats to the top again when you let go.

1 Fill the glass with water. Put a blob of modeling clay on the long spike of the pen top and drop it into the water. You want the pen top to just float so that it is hanging straight down in the water with the tip at the surface. Add or take away clay until you have it just right. (If you haven't got this type of pen top, make a ring of clay all around the end of the cap so that it is balanced and floats vertically in the water.)

You will need:

A glass

Some modeling clay

A ballpoint pen top—without a hole at the end (the best ones are ones with long side spikes)

A 2 quart (2 liter) clear plastic bottle

Water

Tip

To make your diver more realistic, cut out a small diver figure (about the same size as the pen top) from a piece of foil tray. Attach him to the cap with a small paper clip. Test how the cap floats in the glass before you put him in the bottle, adding or taking away clay if you need to.

2 It's best to do this part in the sink! Fill the bottle right to the very top and then drop in the "diver." The water should be level with the top of the plastic. Screw on the lid.

The science

BEHIND THE MAGIC

Squeezing the bottle forces the water into the pen cap. This means that the diver is more dense, or heavier and it sinks. When the bottle is released, the water moves out of the pen cap. This means the diver is less dense (lighter) so it floats back to the top.

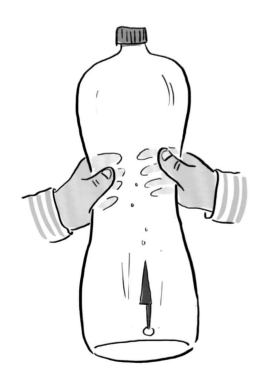

3 Gently squeeze the bottle. The pen cap diver will immediately drop to the bottom of the bottle. Let go and it will float back up again.

Watch it RISE and FALL!

Two ball bounce

Surprise your friends with this very simple trick. It is all to do with the transfer of momentum but what happens is quite unexpected. It's best to do this one outside where nothing can get broken!

You will need:

....

A soccer ball (football) or basketball

A small ball such as a tennis ball or a light rubber ball

1 Hold the two balls, one in each hand, at shoulder height. Drop them at the same time and notice how high each one bounces.

2 Pick the balls up. Hold the large ball in one hand. Place the small ball on top and hold it still with the other hand. Again, hold them out at shoulder height.

How DID that HAPPEN?

3 Let go of both balls together and watch what happens to the small ball!

The science

BEHIND THE MAGIC

The large ball bounces on the ground first and begins to move upward. It hits the smaller ball, which is still coming down and transfers its momentum to the smaller ball, which then shoots high into the air. How much momentum an object has depends on its speed and how heavy it is. The bigger ball has lots of momentum to transfer to the small ball because it is heavy. If you tried this with a big, but very light, inflatable beach ball as the bottom ball, would it work? Try it!

Hook up the circuits and see your friends jump! You simply set up a buzzer circuit and attach it to different switches. The first switch will set off the buzzer when someone closes the bathroom door. The second sets off the buzzer when someone steps on a mat. The third triggers the buzzer with a tilt switch in a cookie tin.

You will need:

Wires—some of them quite long

Battery pack and batteries

Buzzer

Cardboard

Scissors

Large paper clips

Sticky tape

Small sponge

Cardboard candy tube, or other small tube with one cardboard end

Small sharp scissors and cutting board

Brads (paper fasteners)

A large metal ball bearing (or a medium sized marble and some aluminum foil)

A rectangular tin or box with a lid

Paper and pen

Bathroom door switch

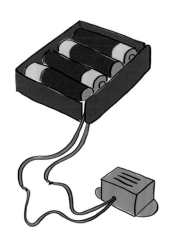

1 First set up a simple circuit with wires, a battery packs and a buzzer. If your circuit does not work turn the buzzer around so that it is connected the other way around – buzzers only work one way in a circuit. Once it works, disconnect it so that you don't run down the batteries.

2 To make the switch for the bathroom door, first cut a rectangle of cardboard about 3½ x 2 inches (9 x 5 cm). Fold it in the middle, bringing short end to meet short end.

SURPRISE your FRIENDS!

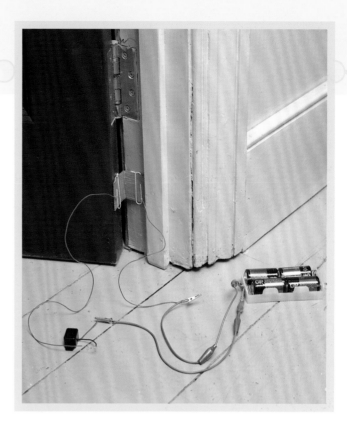

3 Push a paper clip onto each short end of the cardboard. Attach a long wire to each of the paper clips.

4 With the bathroom door open, use sticky tape to fix the switch below the inside bottom door hinge, so the switch is like a hinge, with half on the door and half on the frame. When the door closes the two halves of cardboard will close together and the two paperclips should touch each other. Be careful no one closes the door while you are setting up your switch—you don't want your fingers to get trapped.

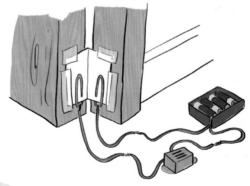

5 Join the wires from the paper clips to the wires of your circuit to make one big circuit. Test it works. When you close the door the paper clips will touch and complete the circuit and the buzzer will buzz loudly! Try to hide the battery and buzzer so that whoever next uses the bathroom doesn't see it!

Under the mat switch

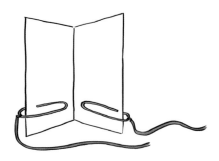

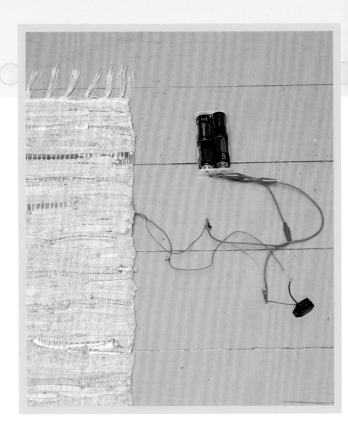

1 Follow steps 1–3 of the instructions for the bathroom door switch but this time push the paper clips across the cardboard, so they cover the width of the cardboard.

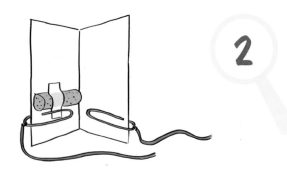

2 Cut a strip of sponge about ½ x ½ inches (1 x 1 cm) and as long as the paper clips. Tape the sponge just beside one of the paper clips, on the side nearest to the fold. It might be easiest to take off the paper clip while you tape it on and then put it back. The sponge should stop the paper clips touching when you close the cardboard gently.

3 Put the switch under a mat in the place where you think someone is most likely to step. Attach the wires to the buzzer circuit nearby — try to hide it. When someone steps on the mat the sponge will squash flat, the paper clips will touch, and the buzzer will buzz loudly. Step off the mat and the sponge will spring back up and the buzzer will stop.

Cookie tin tilt switch

1   Gently open the cardboard end of the candy tube. Bend it back flat and carefully make two small holes about ½ inch (1 cm) apart in the cardboard, using the end of a sharp pair of scissors and pushing down onto a cutting board.

2   Push a brad (paper fastener) through each of the holes from the inside out. They should be side by side but not touching.

3   The diameter (distance across) of the ball bearing or marble you use should be a bit smaller than the width of the tube. If you are using a ball bearing, drop that into the tube. It must be big enough that when it rolls down the tube it will touch both paper fastener tops at once. (If it is a bit small, wrap it in several layers of foil.) If you are using a marble, wrap it carefully in foil so it is completely covered and drop that in instead.

4   Cut off all the small flaps around the edge of the tube and then tape down the cardboard end of the tube (with the brads) with some sticky tape. The round heads of the brads will now be inside the tube and the pointed ends outside. Make sure that the pointed ends don't touch. Attach wires to the pointed ends.

5 Attach the wires from the brads (paper fasteners) into the buzzer circuit and test the tilt switch. When you tilt the tube, the ball bearing/marble should roll down the tube and touch both brads (paper fasteners) at the same time. This will complete the circuit and the buzzer will go off.

The science
BEHIND THE MAGIC

Electricity only flows in a complete circuit. If there is a gap in the circuit the electricity can't flow. Electricity can also only flow through materials called conductors. These are mostly metals. Electricity can't flow through insulators. Plastic is a good insulator, which is why we cover wires in plastic. The switches create gaps in the circuit. For the first two switches the two paper clips (which are metal and so conduct electricity) need to touch each other to complete the circuit. In the last one the ball bearing (or the foil around the marble) is a conductor, which bridges the gap between the two brads (paper fasteners) and so completes the circuit.

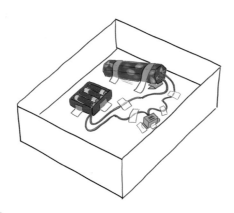

6 Tape the tube to the inside of the cookie tin. Raise the brad (paper fastener) end slightly on some cardboard so the marble doesn't roll too soon. Tape the rest of the circuit into the tin.

7 To make sure your victim lifts up the tin and tilts it, write a label to put on the side of the tin opposite where the brads (paper fasteners) are. How about: WARNING: READ CAREFULLY BEFORE OPENING! Your victim will pick up the tin, tilt it up to read it, and the buzzer should buzz! Finally put on the cookie tin lid and invite your victim to eat a cookie from the tin.

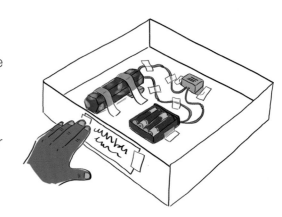

Wobbly clown and back-flipping clown

The first clown wibbles and wobbles but will never lie down.
The second one does back flips all the way down a slope.

Wobbly clown

You will need:

....

A table tennis ball

Pointed scissors

Cardstock

Newspaper

Sticky tape

Marker pens

Modeling clay

A big marble

1 First cut the table tennis ball in half around the join line of the ball. You may need to ask an adult to help you cut it.

2 Cut a rectangle of cardstock that is 5 x 3 inches (12 x 8 cm).

3 Tightly roll up a piece of newspaper so that it is the same diameter as the table tennis ball and tuck the roll inside one of the ball halves (this is to make the next stage easier).

4 Cut a piece of sticky tape ready to use. Wrap the rectangle of cardstock around the newspaper and ball half and tape the cardstock together to make a tube.

 5 Now tape around the join between the cardboard tube and the ball.

6 With the newspaper roll still inside to press against while you draw, draw a silly clown's face on the cardboard. Then take out the newspaper and try to stand him up. You'll find it is impossible!

 7 Now roll some modeling clay into a ball that's a bit smaller than the half table tennis ball and drop it through the tube. Press it down so it sticks inside the bottom of the ball – you could use a pencil to push it down. Try standing your clown up now. You'll find he stands up easily but when you push him over he just pops up again—he won't stay lying down!

The CLOWN that WON'T LIE DOWN

Back-flipping clown

1 Take the modeling clay out of your wobbly clown and drop in the marble instead.

2 Tape the other half of the table tennis ball to the top of the cardboard tube.

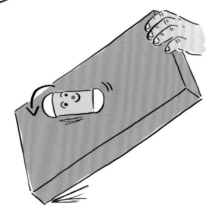

3 Stand the clown at the top of a slight slope and give it a flick. Watch the clown do back flips all the way down the slope.

The science

BEHIND THE MAGIC

Gravity always pulls objects down toward the center of the Earth. In the clown with the modeling clay inside, almost all the weight is at the bottom—gravity pulls the bottom down and the clown stands upright. Because of its curved bottom, when you knock it over, with gravity still pulling the weight down, the clown's head flips up again. When you have the marble instead of the modeling clay inside, as soon as the clown starts moving the marble inside rolls from one end to the other, pulling first one end down and then the other, so he flips!

There-and-back roller

Roll the can along the floor—it stops and then, just like magic, rolls back to where it started. It's all to do with stored energy!

You will need:

....

A hammer

A nail

A board

An empty can with a plastic or metal fitted lid (coffee or cocoa cans are good)

Lots of rubber bands (or a long piece of elastic)

A plastic bag

Scissors

A small weight

Thin string

1 You will need to ask an adult to help you with this step. Use the hammer, nail, and board to punch two holes about 1 inch (2.5 cm) apart in the bottom of the can and two more in the lid. (Watch your fingers when you do this and watch for sharp edges around the holes when you punch through metal.) The holes should be big enough to thread a piece of elastic or a rubber band through.

2 Link the rubber bands together to make one long chain as follows: put one band half on top of another. Bring the end of the bottom band up through the top band and thread the other end of the bottom band through the loop you have made. Pull it tight and link the next band in the same way (or you can use one long piece of elastic).

3 Make a little bag for your weight. Cut a square of plastic bag, put the weight on top, gather the plastic up around it and tie it tightly with some thin string. Make a small loop of string at the top.

4 Thread the two ends of the rubber band chain/elastic through the two holes at the bottom of the can.

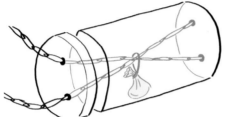

The science
BEHIND THE MAGIC

As the can rolls away from you the weight inside the can twists the elastic band. Energy is stored in the twisted band, which wants to push in the opposite direction to the way the can is moving. The energy builds up until the can stops and then it pushes the can back the way it has come.

5 Inside the can, thread the weight onto the rubber band chain/elastic. Cross the two ends of the rubber band chain/elastic and thread them through the holes in the lid.

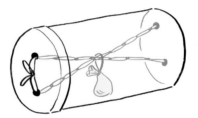

6 Now put the lid on the can and then pull through the ends of the rubber band chain/elastic and tie them together with a knot. The rubber band chain/elastic shouldn't be loose in the can but it shouldn't be too stretched either.

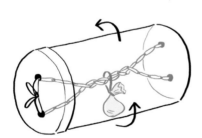

7 Roll the can away from you and wait for it to come rolling back!

Off it goes—BACK IT COMES!

Balloon rocket

This balloon rocket is easy to make but it really does go! Try making one it your backyard with a good long piece of kite string or fishing line, or you can do it indoors, but get an adult's permission first! This project is much easier with a friend to help you.

You will need:

About 16 feet (4.5 meters) of kite string or fishing line—the smoother the string, the faster your rocket will go

A plastic drinking straw

A balloon—the long torpedo-shaped ones are best

A balloon pump (optional)

Sticky tape

1 Choose two objects to tie the string to—for example, garden chairs, trees, or fences. They should be about 10–15 feet (3–5 meters) apart, but they don't have to be at exactly the same height—your rocket can fly uphill or downhill. Tie one end of the string to one of the objects.

2 Thread the other end of the string through the drinking straw.

3 Now get your friend to help you pull the string as tight as possible while you tie it to the other object.

Investigate your rocket design

You can launch your rocket over and over again and use a stopwatch to time the results. Try it with different shaped balloons—which shape goes fastest or furthest? Try different types of string—which string makes the rocket go fastest or furthest? Does the angle of the string make a difference? Does the length of the straw make a difference?

4 Blow up the balloon—using a balloon pump if you have one—but don't knot it. Twist the end and hold it closed while your friend tapes the straw to the balloon in two different places. The balloon opening will be the back of the rocket so make sure the front is facing along the string.

5 Launch your rocket; simply let the end of the balloon go and see it shoot along the string!

The science
BEHIND THE MAGIC

Stand on a skateboard and push against a wall—what happens? You move backward! A very famous scientist called Isaac Newton said that "for every action there is an equal and opposite reaction." In other words, you push on the wall and the wall pushes back on you. In the balloon rocket, the air has been forced into the stretchy balloon, which is trying to squeeze it out again. When you let go of the end of the balloon, the air is forced out very quickly—pushing one way—so the balloon moves the opposite way. This forward motion is called THRUST. In a real rocket, thrust is created by the force of burning rocket fuel as it blasts from the rocket's engine—as the engines blast down, the rocket goes up!

Watch it go WHOOSH!

Ice cream science

On the whole, eating and science projects don't mix—you should never taste anything in a science laboratory—but in this project you can use the power of salt to freeze your own ice cream and then you can eat it! Even better, if you are doing this in the winter and there is snow on the ground, you can use snow from your backyard instead of the ice cubes!

You will need:

....

For the ice cream mix:

½ cup (120 ml) milk

½ cup (120 ml) heavy (double) cream

¼ cup (50 g) sugar

¼ teaspoon vanilla extract

Measuring cup and spoon

Pitcher (jug)

Spoon for stirring

To freeze the ice cream:

1-quart (2-pint) zip-lock freezer bag, about 7 x 8 inches (18 x 20 cm)

A pair of warm gloves

2–3 cups of ice cubes

A clean tea towel

A rolling pin

1-gallon (8-pint) zip-lock freezer bag, about 10 x 11 inches (25 x 27.5 cm)

Thermometer (optional)

½–¾ cup (120–180 g) salt

1 Put the milk, cream, sugar, and vanilla extract into the jug and give everything a good stir.

2 Pour this ice cream mixture into the smaller zip-lock bag, squeeze out the air, and zip it closed.

3 Put on your gloves and ask an adult to help you take ice cubes from the freezer. (Don't touch them with bare hands or they could stick to your skin and hurt it.) Pile the ice cubes onto a clean tea towel. Wrap them up and gently bash them with a rolling pin to crush them.

4 Put about 2 cups of crushed ice (or snow) into the large zip-lock bag. If you have a thermometer, measure the temperature of the ice.

5 Add the salt to the ice and, with your gloves still on, mush the outside of the bag a bit to mix the salt and ice.

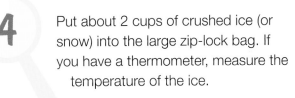

The science
BEHIND THE MAGIC

Ice needs energy (heat) to change from a solid to a liquid. If you put plain ice around the ice cream mix, the ice would take warmth from the mix and cool it—but not enough to freeze it. Salt lowers the freezing point of ice, so if you add salt to ice it will need even more energy (heat) to melt it. It takes all this energy from the ice cream, making it cold enough to freeze into ice cream. When you measure the temperature of the ice the second time, it will be much lower than the first time!

6 Still with your gloves on, put the bag with ice cream mix in it inside the bag with the ice. Make sure the smaller bag is surrounded by ice and salt. Squeeze out the air and zip seal the big bag. Still wearing gloves, gently squeeze and massage the ice around the inner bag. Keep doing this for about 10–15 minutes.

7 Check it! The ice cream mix in the inner bag will have frozen into ice cream, even though you haven't put it in the freezer! Still wearing gloves, take the ice cream bag out of the bigger bag. Measure the temperature of the ice again and then eat your ice cream!

MASH UP some ICE CREAM

Water rocket

5 — 4 — 3 — 2 — 1 blast off! You will not believe how high you can make a plastic bottle fly or the feeling of suspense as you wait for it to launch. To make a water rocket you will have to buy a Rokit kit (or ask for one for a birthday present) but it is well worth it and it can be used over and over again.

You will need:

A Rokit water rocket kit (see page 112)

A bucket of water and a pitcher (jug)

A large plastic fizzy drink bottle (1 or 2-quart/liter is ideal)—check that the Rokit collar fits the bottle

A bicycle pump (a floor pump is best)

A large, safe, open area for launching—check that there are no overhead power lines

A stopwatch (optional)

1 Always ask an adult to help you. Following the instructions in the Rokit kit, put together the parts of the collar and attach the fins to it. Pour water into the bottle until it is about a quarter full and screw on the collar. Attach the screw end of the yellow pressure tube to a bicycle pump and push the brass plug, on the other end, into the hole in the black rubber nozzle in the collar.

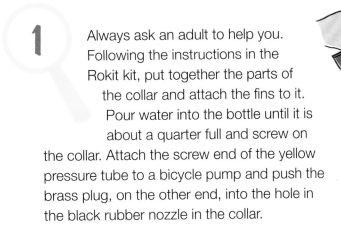

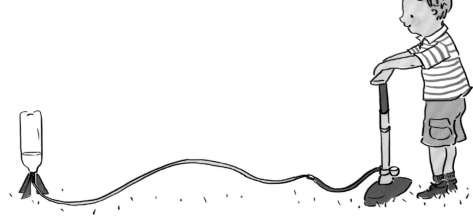

2 Turn the rocket over so it is standing on its fins and position on some firm, flat ground. Step back as far as you can—the hose is quite long—and begin pumping. You will see the air bubbling up through the water but it is hard to guess when the rocket will take off! If you are too close you will get showered with water.

3 Now you can begin some real science. It is quite difficult to measure how high the rocket goes but you can time how long it stays in the air. You and your friends could hold a competition. You could each make a custom-built rocket and then see which one stays up for longest. Try adding a nose cone or bigger fins. Can you design a parachute that will let it drop back to earth more slowly? Is it better to have more water or less water in the bottle?

The science
BEHIND THE MAGIC

When you pump air into the bottle the pressure inside rises. It keeps rising until it is strong enough to force the end of the hose out through the rubber nozzle. The water is also forced out of the hole in the nozzle. The force of the water pushing downward produces thrust in the opposite direction (see page 63) so the rocket shoots up against the force of gravity. After a few seconds the thrust gets weaker until gravity is as strong as the thrust so the rocket reaches its highest point. Then gravity pulls the rocket back down to earth. A parachute would slow the rocket down by increasing air resistance. A nose cone could make the rocket more streamlined so it might go higher. The fins add stability so it flies straighter.

We have **LIFT OFF!**

Freshwater wizardry

Imagine being adrift on the ocean or stranded on a desert island with no fresh water. Here's a bit of science that could help you survive, although you might not have quite the same equipment in your boat or on your island! This is a project to do outside on a hot, sunny day.

1 Ask permission to use the bowl first and be very careful not to drop it. A glass or china bowl is better than plastic because the plastic wrap will cling to it. Find a hot sunny place to put the bowl, where it won't be in the way or get knocked over. Place the glass in the middle of the bowl.

You will need:

A large glass or china bowl—a glass one will make it easier to see what is going on

A small glass—not as tall as the bowl

A pitcher (jug)

Water

A tablespoon

Salt

Spoon for stirring

Plastic wrap (cling film)

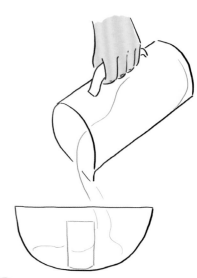

2 Fill the pitcher (jug) with water and add several tablespoons of salt. Stir the water well to dissolve the salt.

3 Pour the water into the bowl around the glass.

The science
BEHIND THE MAGIC

Because of the heat from the sun, some of the water in the bowl evaporates to become water vapor. The salt that is dissolved in the water cannot evaporate. The air above the plastic wrap (cling film) will be cooler than the air in the bowl so when the water vapor touches the plastic wrap it cools and condenses back into liquid water—just like when you get condensation on a cold glass in the summer. The condensation runs down to the center of the bowl and drips into the glass—fresh water!

4 Cover the bowl with plastic wrap (cling film), making sure that it is sealed so that no air can get in or out.

5 Gently press down in the center of the plastic wrap (cling film) above the glass to make the plastic dip down a little there. Be careful not to make a hole.

6 Leave the bowl all day or for several days. Fresh, unsalty water will slowly collect in the glass.

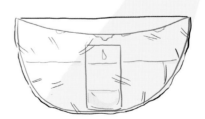

Learn a SURVIVAL technique

Making rainbows

Think about all the many different places you have seen rainbows: up in the sky when the sun is shining after a storm; in a puddle covered with a film of oil; in bubbles; on CDs left in the sun; on the walls of your house when the sun is shining through a hanging crystal or a crystal vase. Can you think of any other places you have seen them? This project shows you two ways to make rainbows of your own.

You will need:

....

A garden hose

A sunny day

or

A flashlight (torch)

Black paper

Pencil

Scissors

Sticky tape

A plastic food box

Water

A small mirror—a purse mirror is ideal

White card

Sunny day method

1 The first way of making a rainbow is with a hose on a hot sunny day. Stand with your back to the sun. Put your finger over the end of the hose so the water comes out in a fine spray—or you may have a spray nozzle on the hose that you can use instead. Look into the spray and find the rainbow!

Indoor method

1 If it is not hot and sunny, make a rainbow in a dark room or even inside a dark cupboard! Put the flashlight (torch) face down on a piece of black paper and use a pencil to draw around the face of the flashlight.

2 Cut out the circle. Fold the circle in half and cut out a tiny hole in the middle. Tape the circle over the face of the flashlight (torch).

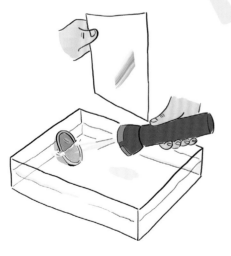

3 Half fill the box with water and stand the mirror in the box so that it is leaning against one end at an angle, half in the water.

4 Switch out all the lights. Shine the flashlight through the water onto the part of the mirror that is underwater.

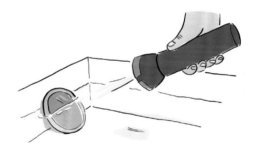

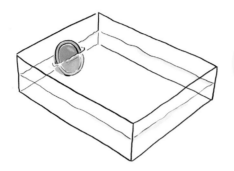

5 Hold the white cardboard up to catch the light that is reflecting off the mirror—look for the rainbow!

"RED and YELLOW and PINK and GREEN..."

Make your own compass

Magnets are cool—you can have a lot of fun playing with them. If you haven't got a set you might find some stuck to your fridge! Try and get two (not the bendy fridge ones) and find out a bit about them first. Then go on to make a compass by using a magnet you have made yourself.

1 First have a play with your two magnets. Bring them together. Do the ends stick easily (attract) or push each other away (repel)? How strong are they? You can check by finding out how many pins or paper clips they can lift. Can you move a metal object on top of a table with a magnet held underneath?

You will need:
....

Two bar magnets

A sewing needle

A few pins or paper clips

A plastic bottle top

A little adhesive putty (Blu-Tack®)

A shallow bowl of water

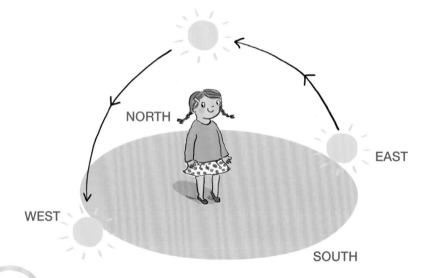

2 Now see if you can work out where north is without a compass. Do you know where the sun rises? That direction is east. Think where it sets—that's west. If you live in the Northern Hemisphere (that includes the USA and the UK) and you go outside at midday on a sunny day, your shadow will point north.

3 Time to make a compass! Take one magnet. The ends of a magnet are called poles. On bar magnets the ends may be labeled N for north pole and S for south pole or the north pole may be painted red. Use the north pole of the magnet to stroke along the needle from the eye to the point. Lift the magnet in a circle away from the needle each time. Do this about 20 times.

The science

BEHIND THE MAGIC

Imagine that inside the steel needle there are lots of tiny magnets but they are all pointing in different directions so they cancel each other out. When you stroke them with a stronger magnet they are all pulled into line and work together to make one big magnet.
The Earth acts as if it has a gigantic bar magnet running through it but the magnet's south pole is near what we call the North Pole (where Santa lives!). You found, when playing with magnets, that opposite poles attract each other, so the north pole of a magnetized needle is attracted toward the North Pole of the Earth (which is really the south pole of the Earth's magnet—so it's all a bit confusing!)

4 Check that you have turned your needle into a magnet—try lifting a few pins with it. Do more stroking if it can't hold any pins.

5 Turn the bottle top upside down to make a little boat and lay the needle across the center—a little adhesive putty (Blu-Tack®) stuck to the rim on each side will keep it in place.

6 Float the bottle top on the water in the bowl. The top will turn slowly back and forth until it settles with the point of the needle pointing north—or it will if you used the north pole of the magnet to magnetize your needle! If you didn't know which was which and have used the south pole of the magnet instead, the eye of the needle will be pointing north.
It doesn't really matter—the important thing is that one end points in the direction that you worked out was north. Does it? If it does, you have made a compass!

chapter 3
Backyard Biology

Pop-up glove

Question: How do you get the air holes in bread, which make it look like sponge?
Answer: By using yeast. Yeast is a microorganism (a living thing that is too small to be seen with the naked eye). When we mix it with flour, sugar, water, and salt to make bread it feeds off the sugar and produces the gas carbon dioxide. This is what makes bubbles in the bread dough. But yeast is a bit like Goldilocks in the story of the Three Bears. It doesn't like things too hot or too cold; they need to be just right. You can see this by watching the gloves in this experiment. If the yeast produces carbon dioxide gas it will inflate the glove to make a pop-up hand on top of the cup!

You will need:

3 small transparent plastic cups (the gloves should fit tightly over the top of the cups)

3 sticky labels

Active dried yeast (for baking)

A measuring teaspoon (5 ml)

Sugar

Water

A measuring pitcher (jug)

A spoon for stirring

A waterproof tray

3 latex gloves (the type doctors use)

1 Label the cups 1, 2, and 3.

2 Put one teaspoon of dried yeast into each cup. Each teaspoon of dried yeast contains millions of microscopic yeast cells!

3 Add two teaspoons of sugar to each cup.

4 Ask an adult to boil some water in a kettle and then let it cool for about 5 minutes so that it is still quite hot, but not boiling.

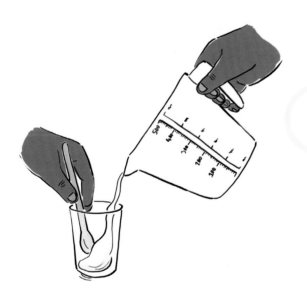

5 Measure ½ cup (100 ml) of cold water into the measuring pitcher (jug), pour it into cup 1, and stir it well.

6 Now measure about ⅓ cup (70 ml) of cold water into the pitcher (jug) and then very carefully add hot water until you have ½ cup (100 ml). The water should be cool enough to put your finger into comfortably. Pour this into cup 2 and stir well.

7 Lastly, very carefully measure ½ cup (100 ml) of hot water and pour it into cup 3. Stir it well.

8 Making sure that you don't spill the mixture, carefully put a glove over the top of each cup. Stand the cups together on a tray.

9 Now you need to wait. Watch carefully to see if you can see any bubbles forming in the mixtures or any froth on the top. Froth will show that the yeast is feeding on the sugar and making bubbles of carbon dioxide. Keep checking every 10 minutes to see what is happening. You could leave the experiment for several hours or even overnight. Which of the gloves do you think will popup? What do you think might happen to the yeast in cup 3 with the very hot water? What do you think will happen with the cold water?

The science
BEHIND THE MAGIC

The water activates the dried yeast, bringing it back to life (because all living things need water). The yeast then feeds on the sugar and, as a waste product, produces carbon dioxide, which inflates the glove. Because yeast is living it needs to be at a certain temperature to be properly alive and active. The best temperature for activating yeast is 105–115°F (41–46°C). Very hot water will kill the yeast.

Watch the **GHOSTLY** hand **RISE UP!**

10 ways to find out about snails

Snails are fascinating creatures and in this project you are going to investigate them in ten mini-projects. Snails are very easy to find but remember that snails are living things and deserve to be treated gently and with respect, just like any other creature. Also, always remember to wash your hands after you've been exploring outside.

You will need:

A large glass jar—take care not to drop it

Plastic wrap (cling film)

Rubber band

Pencil

A magnifying glass

Cornstarch (cornflour)

Small paintbrush

Plate

Q-tip (cotton bud)

A flashlight (torch)

Vinegar

A sharp knife—ask an adult!

Small amounts of some of these snail "foods": sawdust, lettuce, oatmeal, apple, milk, cardboard, orange, carrot

A plastic or metal cake box

Sticky tape

Chalk

Brightly colored nail polish

1 **Find some snails** Snails come out mostly at night but they will still be around on damp, cloudy mornings. On sunny days you will find them hiding in their shells in damp, dark places. Put four or five snails into a large glass jar. Put a few wet leaves and a little damp soil in the jar with them to make them comfortable! To keep them inside, cover the top with plastic wrap (cling film). Keep it firm with a rubber band and make a few tiny holes with the point of a pencil to give them air. You will be surprised at how quickly they can escape if you leave the jar open!

2 **How do snails move?** Take the jar to a cool, shady spot and wait for them to come out of their shells. Watch as a snail crawls up the glass of the jar. Look out for dark ripples moving along its "foot." These are its muscles, which push it along. Look for the trail of slime it leaves as it moves. You may also see it doing a poo as it crawls along! Use the magnifying glass to look closer. Look for a hole near the entrance to its shell. This is the snail's breathing hole.

3 How do snails eat? Mix a little cornstarch (cornflour) with some water to make a thin paste. Remove the plastic wrap (cling film) cover from the jar and use a paintbrush to brush a patch of this paste onto the side of the jar. Watch carefully as the snail eats it—snails love cornstarch (cornflour)! Use the magnifying glass to see more clearly. You should be able to see the snail's mouth eating. It has something called a radula, which is like a rough tongue with rows and rows of tiny teeth. It uses the radula to scrape the surface off leaves—a bit like sandpaper. Can you see marks in the cornstarch (corn flour) where the radula has scraped?

4 Can snails learn? Take a snail out of the jar and put it on the plate. (Remember to shut the others in!) Wet the Q-tip (cotton bud) and then very gently touch its head behind its tentacles. What happens to the tentacles? How long do they take to come back out again? Leave the snail to move around a bit more, then touch it again. Do this five or six times. After a while you may find that the snail does not take much notice when it is touched. It has learned that nothing bad happens so it is not in danger.

5 **Can snails see and hear?** Shine the flashlight (torch) at the snail. Does it react? Its upper, longer tentacles react to light and dark, but the snail can't see in the same way as we can. Try whistling or clapping near the snail. Does it react when you make a noise? Snails can't hear so it shouldn't notice the noise you make.

6 **Can snails smell?** Clean the paintbrush then use it to paint a circle of vinegar around the snail (not too close). Watch what happens as it crawls toward the vinegar. Its lower tentacles can smell. Does it like the smell of vinegar?

7 **Why do snails make slime trails?** Ask an adult if you can use a sharp knife. Wash the vinegar off the plate and lay the knife flat on the plate. Let the snail crawl onto it (brush on some cornstarch (cornflour) paste to tempt it if it doesn't move). When the snail is on the knife, turn the knife so that the sharp blade is facing up and the snail has to climb over it. It sounds cruel but it won't cut the snail! Its slime will protect it. In the wild the slime protects snails from sharp thorns and helps them glide over rough surfaces. It also stops them from drying out.

SNAIL TRAILS and other SECRETS

8 **What is a snail's favorite food?** Let's find out! Put samples of different foods around the edges of a large plastic box. Include damp sawdust, damp cardboard, lettuce, apple slices, cornstarch (cornflour) paste, oatmeal, and a little milk. You could try other fruit and vegetables too but don't include processed sugary or salty foods as these are poisonous to snails. Put all your snails into the middle of the box. Cover the top of the box with plastic wrap (cling film), pierce a few tiny holes in the top with a pencil, and hold it down with a large rubber band or some sticky tape. Now wait and watch. Keep checking every few minutes to see which foods the snails end up on. Is there a clear favorite or do all the snails end up on different foods? Leave them overnight. Which foods have been eaten?

9 **Snail race** This part is best done with a few friends. Make a racecourse on a hard surface such as a patio, but make sure you choose a shady, damp corner as snails hate to be dry or out in the sun. Use chalk to draw a large circle and put all the snails in the middle. Each of you should pick a snail. Whose snail will reach the edge first? Can you encourage your snail to go faster or straighter with different foods?

10 **Snail hunt** Gather your snails together—you could perhaps collect some more snails to make this activity even more fun. Mark each snail with a blob of colored nail polish. In the evening, take all the snails to the middle of your backyard and let them go. The next morning, set out for a snail hunt and see how many of your marked snails you can find. How far did they travel in a night? You will probably keep finding your snails over the next weeks, months, or even years as some snails live for a long time! You could also try putting one of your marked snails in your neighbor's yard (you must ask for permission first). You may well find that it has returned to your yard overnight—this is because snails have a homing instinct.

You will need:

A trowel

A coffee or baby formula can—or any other metal can with a plastic top

A piece of wooden board or a tile that is bigger than the can

Four pebbles or stones—all about the same size

A tray with steep sides or a wide shallow box

White paper

A bug pot with a magnifying lens, or a magnifying glass

A book to help you identify your catches (optional)

Notebook and pencil

You have probably read stories in which animals are trapped when they fall into holes disguised by branches and leaves. A pitfall trap is just like that but smaller. By setting one up in your backyard, you will be able to catch and investigate some of the fascinating bugs that scuttle around on the ground when you're not looking!

SAFETY

Always wash your hands after you have been exploring outside.

1 Decide where to dig your trap. Choose a damp place, where the soil is soft enough to dig, among trees and bushes or near old logs. This is the kind of place where lots of bugs and beetles crawl around, especially at night.

2 Dig a hole as big as the can and put your can into it. Fill up any gaps around the can with loose soil so that the can fits snugly in the hole with the rim just below soil level. If there is any rim showing above the soil the bugs will simply walk around the rim!

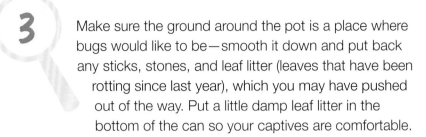

3 Make sure the ground around the pot is a place where bugs would like to be—smooth it down and put back any sticks, stones, and leaf litter (leaves that have been rotting since last year), which you may have pushed out of the way. Put a little damp leaf litter in the bottom of the can so your captives are comfortable.

4 Put the board over the top of the can and then place a stone under each corner to hold the board just above the ground. This way the bugs will crawl under the board and fall into the trap. It will be cool and shady underneath in the daytime and the board will also keep out rain.

5 Leave the trap for 24 hours. Before you check it, cover the bottom of the tray or box with white paper. Then, take out the can and tip your catch into the tray. Be careful not to let any captives escape—some beetles move very quickly! The bugs will show up clearly on the white surface. See how many different bugs you have caught.

6 Use the bug pot or magnifying glass to examine each one more closely. How many can you identify? A good scientist will record what they have found in a notebook.

7 Once you have had a good look, put all the bugs and beetles back on the ground, near the trap.

The science

BEHIND THE MAGIC

The correct name for a bug is an invertebrate, which means an animal without a backbone. Invertebrates have no skeletons inside their bodies but may have a hard outside called an *exoskeleton*. Spiders and insects have exoskeletons but slugs and worms have no hard parts at all. There may be hundreds of different invertebrates scuttling or creeping around your yard, especially at night. Even though many are good climbers, if they fall into your trap their feet will not be able to grip on the smooth wall of the coffee can so they will be trapped.

8 You might want to set up the trap just once, in which case fill the hole back up with soil. If you want to try several times, put the can back but you must check it every 24 hours so that creatures (including small frogs and toads) don't get left in the trap with no food or water. If you are not going to be able check it, or if it is going to rain hard (which could drown your captives) put the lid on the can. You can take it off again when you next want to use the trap.

Trap yourself a WILD BEASTIE!

Get to know a tree

Scientists who study plants and animals often need to watch them for a long time to see how they change or what happens to them in different seasons. The other projects in this book are mostly pretty quick but this one is all about taking time. Take time to get to know a tree because trees are amazing. If you really want to be a scientist, see if you have the sticking power to record what happens to a favourite tree over a whole year. Take photos, write notes, draw pictures and end up with a really special diary.

SAFETY

Always wash your hands after you have been exploring outside.

You will need:

A favorite tree

Tree identification guide

A special notebook

Pencil

Blindfold

Wax crayon

Paper—thin is best

Camera and printer

Glue stick

Teaspoon

Bug pot

1 **Choose a tree** Choose one in your backyard or nearby in a park or in the wild. Choose one you think is special perhaps because of its shape or because it's really tall or even better because it has a few low branches so that you can climb it. A deciduous tree is one that loses its leaves in the fall (autumn) and is probably more interesting than an evergreen because there will be more changes to record. Identify your tree by using your guide. This is easier in the summer when the trees have their leaves. Look at the shape and size of the tree, the shape of its leaves, and what sort of seeds it has to help you find what type of tree it is.

2 **Hug your tree** If there are a few other trees near to your tree this is a fun activity, but you will need someone to help you. Start by looking at your tree really carefully. Look at where the lowest branches are. Look at how wide the trunk it. Look at how rough the bark is and any special marks on it. Ask the other person to blindfold you, to turn you around a few times so you don't know where you are, then to lead you to a tree. Now you need to hug the tree, to feel it all over and to try and decide whether or not it is your chosen tree! If it isn't your tree, get the other person to take you to your tree so you can hug it and get to know it through touch. Write a few words about it in your notebook.

3 **Make bark and leaf rubbings** Peel the paper off a wax crayon. Hold a piece of paper against the tree trunk and rub over it with the side of the crayon. You will see the pattern of the bark on the paper. Do some leaf rubbings in a similar way. Put a leaf on a table with the veiny side up. Cover it with paper and rub with the side of the wax crayon. Neatly cut out the best section of bark rubbing and the best leaf rubbings and stick them in your notebook.

Hug a TREE today

4 **Start your tree diary** Try to notice your tree every day as you walk to school or play in your backyard. Watch for changes each season brings and record them in your notebook. Look for these changes: When do the leaves start to change color? When in the fall (autumn) are they most colorful? When are there no leaves left? When does the first leaf bud split open in spring? When are all the leaves fully open? When do you see the first flowers and what do they look like? (Yes, trees have flowers too!) When do the nuts, berries, or other type of seeds look ripe and ready for squirrels or birds to eat? What does your tree look like in the snow? Has your tree lost any branches in a storm? Each time you see a change in your tree, take a photo and stick it in your diary with the date and a few notes.

5 **Do a wildlife survey** Search all around your tree for the creatures that live there. Dig around the roots for beetles and worms. Check all the nooks and crannies in the bark for spiders, snails, and other bugs. Check leaves for caterpillars. Use the teaspoon to catch interesting bugs in your bug pot for a closer look but remember to let them go again. Sit under your tree, or in a branch if it is safe to climb, and watch to see if birds or other animals visit your tree. Make a list of everything you see there.

The science
BEHIND THE MAGIC

See if you can find out more about how amazing trees are and how much we need them. Trees give us shade, shelter, wood to build, fuel for fires, fruit and nuts to eat. They take carbon dioxide out of the atmosphere and put back oxygen, which we need to breathe. Their leaves turn into soil to grow our food and their roots stop soil from being washed away. They are also home to many, many other creatures.

6 **Visit your tree at night** Ask an adult to take you to watch your tree on a clear night. Listen to the sounds around your tree at night. There may be owls out hunting or bats flying around. In winter try taking a photo of the moon through the branches.

Stop motion bean pot

Ever wondered what happens to seeds after you've planted them in the ground? Now you can find out with these stop-motion bean pots. They will show you the stages of germination and you will be rewarded with a bean plant ready to put in the garden.

You will need:

A cardboard tube

Newspaper

Sticky tape

Potting mix (compost)

A clear plastic pint-sized beaker

Colored paper napkins

Pole/Runner or green (climbing French) bean seeds. Instead of runner beans you could grow other types of beans— French beans, fava (broad) beans, or borlotti beans. Only climbing beans will need a cane for support

A small pitcher (jug)

A hand trowel

Bamboo cane

A watering can

1 Place the cardboard tube end down on a double layer of newspaper. Now gather up the newspaper around the tube and secure it with sticky tape. It doesn't have to be neat but one end of the tube must be sealed.

2 Carefully fill the tube with some potting mix (compost), making sure that you firm it down inside the tube as you go (but don't push it through the paper end!). Place the tube in the plastic beaker and stuff paper napkins in the space between the tube and the sides of the beaker.

WATCH how SEEDS grow!

3 Use your finger to make a hole about 1½ inches (4 cm) deep in the potting mix (compost). Plant a bean seed in the hole, cover it over with more potting mix (compost), and then firm it down. Try not to spill any over the side of the tube.

4 Push another bean seed about 1½ inches (4 cm) down the side of the beaker between the beaker and the napkin so that you can see it clearly from the outside.

5 With a small pitcher (jug), slowly add water to the tube and beaker so that the potting mix (compost) and napkins are both damp.

6 After two days, push another bean down the side of the beaker but a little farther along. Keep doing this every two days until you have 6–8 seeds around your pot. Keep the potting mix (compost) and napkins damp. Watch the beans begin to germinate one by one and then, as you turn the beaker around, you will be able to see the whole germination process unfold from start to finish.

7 When the central bean has grown two large leaves and you are certain that there will be no more frosts, take the whole cardboard tube carefully out of the beaker. Find a warm sunny spot in your yard, dig a hole that is as deep as the tube, and place the tube into it. Fill the hole with soil around the tube and firm it down with your hands. The tube will rot away as the bean grows. Water it well.

The science
BEHIND THE MAGIC

Seeds come in all different shapes and sizes but inside every seed is a tiny plant (called an embryo) and a store of food. The hard outside, called the seed case, protects the embryo and stops it drying out. The seed stays dormant (which means it doesn't grow) until it has the right amount of water, air, and warmth. Then the seed case splits and the embryo uses the food store to begin growing. A root grows first, then a shoot, and then the first leaves appear. As soon as the plant has green leaves it can begin to make its own food by photosynthesis (see page 97).

8 Push a garden cane into the soil beside the bean plant—the plant will twine itself around the cane as it grows, but you might want to help it to start climbing by tying it to the cane. Remember, beans are thirsty plants so keep it well watered.

Nature's color palette

A color palette is what artists use to paint a picture. They begin with a few colors and mix them to make many more. Look around you when you are out in your backyard or in the countryside or a park. Nature uses hundreds of different colors in its color palette. In this project you will collect tiny samples of different leaves or flower petals to investigate.

You will need:

Cardboard
Pencil
Ruler
Scissors
Double-sided sticky tape

SAFETY

Always wash your hands after you have been exploring outside.

1 Cut the cardboard into small rectangles about 4 x 2 inches (10 x 5 cm) but don't worry too much about exact sizes as it doesn't really matter too much.

2 Stick rows of double-sided sticky tape to one side of a piece of cardboard so that it is completely covered.

3 Take your cardboard outside and pull the paper backing off the tape to leave a sticky surface (this can be a bit tricky).

A color MOSAIC

4 Decide what you want to investigate. In the fall (autumn) you might want to look at leaf colors. Tear off tiny pieces of leaves about the size of your little fingernail. Start with all the yellows you can find and stick each one to your piece of cardboard. Move into oranges, then reds, then browns so that you have a spectrum of different colors. Cover every space on your cardboard with a mosaic of different-colored leaf pieces.

5 In the spring or summer you could use flower petals instead. One of you could search for pink and red flowers while someone else searches for yellow and orange and someone else for blue and purple—or you could mix all the colors up together. If you only take a fingernail-sized sample of a flower you won't damage it. Never pick whole flowers because then you will be stealing the nectar from the bees and you will stop that flower from making seeds.

The science behind the magic

Inside a leaf are three different color chemicals—one is green, one is yellow, and one is orange. In the summer the green chemical, called chlorophyll, does a very important job. Along with sunlight, water, and carbon dioxide from the air, chlorophyll makes food for the plant in a process called photosynthesis. While this is going on the green color is very strong and hides the other colors. But plants need sunlight to create chlorophyll—without it they turn yellow. With less sun in the fall (autumn), there is less chlorophyll, the green fades, and the yellow and orange colors can be seen. Then as the weather begins to get colder, a layer of cork-like cells grows across the leaf stalks ready for when the leaves fall from the trees. Chemicals are trapped in the leaves and these react with sunlight and turn red.

Flowers are colorful to attract insects (or sometimes even birds or animals). An insect, such as a bee, will settle on a flower to sip nectar from it. While it is visiting, pollen sticks to its body, then the bee flies off in search of more food. It settles on a new flower and the pollen from the last flower rubs off onto the new one. Pollen is needed by the flower to make seeds so the flowers are brightly colored to attract the flying pollinators. Bees are especially attracted to bright blue and violet colors. Hummingbirds prefer red, pink, fuchsia, or purple flowers. Butterflies enjoy bright colors such as yellow, orange, pink, and red.

Brilliant butterflies

Not everyone likes insects or bugs but everyone loves butterflies. It is one of the loveliest sights on a summer day to see butterflies fluttering from flower to flower, sipping nectar. The best way to get butterflies to visit your garden is to plant their favorite flowers but you can also make one of these easy-peasy butterfly feeders and a special insect watering hole. Put them both out in your backyard on a sunny day in summer and see who comes to visit.

You will need:

A ruler

A paper plate

Pencil

Sharp pointy scissors

Colored pens or pencils

String

Mushy fruit

A saucer/tray from under a plant pot

Some small flat pebbles

A pitcher (jug) or watering can

1 First make the butterfly feeder. Place your ruler across the center of the plate and draw a very faint line. Draw a dot at each end ½ inches (1 cm) from the edge of the plate. Turn the ruler and draw another line at right angles to the first one so it makes a cross. Put dots ½ inches (1 cm) from the ends of this line too.

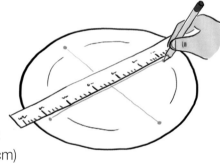

2 Use the point of a pair of sharp scissors to make a hole where you have put each of the four dots.

3 Butterflies prefer white, pink, purple, red, yellow, and orange flowers so decorate your plate in some of these colors. If you want to be a real scientist, make several feeders in different colors and see which the butterflies prefer.

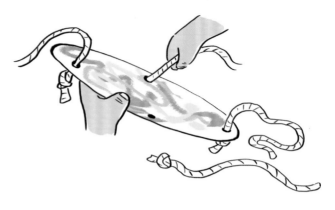

4 Cut four pieces of string each about 11 inches (28 cm) long. Tie a big knot in the end of each piece and thread the other end through each of your four holes.

5 Tie the four pieces together so the plate hangs level like an upside-down parachute.

6 Hang it near some flowers and put some small pieces of mushy fruit onto it. Butterflies really love those mushy bananas that no one else will eat!

Fix up a BUTTERFLY FEAST

Tip

On hot days remember to keep topping up the water in your watering hole so it doesn't dry up.

7 Now for the watering hole. Place the saucer on the ground near your feeder and fill it with a layer of small flat pebbles.

8 Pour water into the tray until it fills the spaces between the stones. The water should not cover the stones. These are for the butterflies to land on.

9 Watch to see how many butterflies or other insects visit your feeder or land in your watering hole for a sip of water.

The science

BEHIND THE MAGIC

Butterflies do not eat; they only suck up liquids with their proboscis, which is a long tube and acts like a straw. When they are not feeding, the proboscis is curled up under their head. (Look out for it on the butterflies that land on your feeder.) They use it to suck nectar out of flowers but also to suck up fruit juice, water, and other liquids. They do not taste with their mouths but with their feet, which have taste sensors on them.

Color-change carnations

Begin with some plain white carnations and change them into any color you like—even multicolored. And it's all because of science, not magic.

You will need:

4 jam jars or glasses

Water

Food coloring in 4 different colors

6 white carnations, or other white flowers with strong stems

Chopping board

A sharp knife (ask an adult to help you)

1 Half-fill all the jam jars with water. Add a different food coloring to each jar. Keep adding drops until the water is a strong color—you'll probably need to add 20–30 drops.

2 Ask an adult to help you. Lay one flower on the chopping board and cut off the end of the stem at a slight diagonal. Do the same with all the flowers.

Turn a WHITE flower BLUE

3 Put one flower in each of the four jars and place them on a bright, sunny windowsill. Push them close together so the jars are touching each other in a line.

4 This next part is a bit tricky and it is easy to cut your fingers, so ask an adult to do it for you. They need to slit the stems of the other two flowers up the middle, but not quite all the way to the top. Stop a couple of inches (about 5 cm) from the head of the flower. Pull the two halves of each stem gently apart.

5 Place the split stems so that one half is in one jar and the other half in the jar next to it. You should end up with one flower with half a stem in the red water and half a stem in the blue water, and the other flower with half a stem in the yellow water and half a stem in the green water.

6 Leave the flowers for 4–6 hours. Keep checking as gradually the flowers change color! What happens to the flowers with the split stems?

The science
BEHIND THE MAGIC

The flowers have a network of tiny tubes in them taking water and food to every cell in the plant. In bright sunlight, water evaporates from the flower petals. This means that more water is sucked up into the tiny tubes that run up the stem. The stem would normally be attached to roots, which would suck up water from the soil but, in this project, the ends of the stems are in the colored water and so this is sucked up into the tubes. As more water evaporates from the flowers the colored water is gradually drawn up through the stems and into the flowers, turning them different colors. The flowers with the split stems will be colored half and half. The red mixed with blue will be half red, half blue, and the yellow mixed with green will be half yellow, half green!

Caterpillar camouflage

If you could ask a bird what its favorite food was, chances are it would say "Caterpillars!" This isn't great news if you are a caterpillar. So caterpillars use all sorts of different ways to stop being eaten. One of these is camouflage. This means they try to blend in with their surroundings so that they can't be spotted. In this fun game you will find out just how well camouflage works.

You will need:

....

Cardboard

Scissors

Double-sided sticky tape

Scraps of wool—some brightly colored, some duller greens and brown

1 This game is more fun if you have some friends to play it with and an adult to help. First cut the cardboard into some long rectangles about 8 x 2 inches (20 x 5 cm). They don't have to be perfect. Have one piece for each player.

2 Stick a length of double-sided sticky tape along the top of the cardboard. Don't peel off the backing paper yet. Write START at one end of the cardboard.

3 Cut the wool into 6 inch (15 cm) lengths. Half the pieces should be brightly colored and half should be green or brown—the colors of leaves and branches. These are your caterpillars! It doesn't really matter how many you cut but for a good game you will need about 20 or more. Count them before you begin the game.

4 While you and your friends stay inside, ask the adult to hide all your "caterpillars" in plants, trees, and bushes around your backyard.

SAFETY

Never touch caterpillars. Many people react badly to them, especially the hairy ones. Always wash your hands after you have been exploring outside.

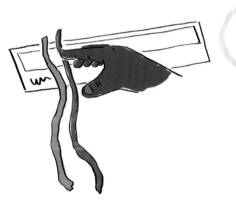

5 Now peel off the backing paper from the sticky tape (this can be a bit tricky) and when the adult says "Ready!", all of you run out and begin searching for the yarn "caterpillars." When you find one, stick it on your cardboard. Stick the first one at the end that says START and line them up in the order in which you find them. Keep going until you have found them all!

6 Count up everyone's caterpillars. If you were birds which of you would have the fullest tummy? Who would still be hungry? Look at the order in which you found your caterpillars. You probably found the bright ones first and the camouflaged ones last. Did you manage to find all the caterpillars or did some survive to turn into butterflies?

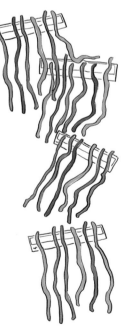

A game of HIDE-AND-SEEK!

Worm charming

You have probably heard of snake charming but have you ever heard of worm charming? Did you know that there is even a World Worm Charming Championship? The point of worm charming is to make as many worms as possible come up out of the ground. This project is a lot of fun, especially if you make it into a competition with some friends.

You will need:

A lawn or field

4 tent pegs or garden skewers for each competitor

A ball of string

A small bucket for each competitor with a covering cloth or lid

Some garden forks and spades

A timer

Big sticks

Musical instruments

A ruler

Weighing scales

A magnifying glass

Prizes or homemade certificates

1 First mark out a plot for each competitor that is about 2 x 2 big paces. Push in a tent peg for one corner of a plot. Take two big paces and push in another tent peg. Turn a corner and take two more paces for the third corner. Keep going to make a square. Stretch string around the tent pegs.

2 Either choose which plot you want (think—where would worms most like to live?) or number the plots and draw numbers out of a hat to choose who has each one. Put a layer of damp soil in each bucket and find a cloth or lid to cover the bucket with.

Where are you, WORMS?!

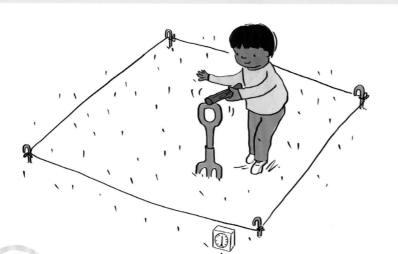

3 The world championship gives the competitor 30 minutes to charm their worms. You could do the same. Set the clock and start charming using any of these charming methods: Push the fork or spade into the ground and bang it to make vibrations; dance all over your plot; drum on the ground with two sticks; use musical instruments to make vibrations; or play your iPod loudly to the grass. What else can you think of?

4 Collect any worms that come to the surface in your bucket. Keep the bucket covered—worms left out in the sun will dry up and die.

5 At the end of half an hour give prizes for the person who has collected:
    the most worms
    the longest worm
    the shortest worm
    the heaviest worm
    the worm with the most segments (the number of rings that make up its body)

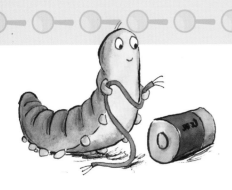

Plants need to produce seeds so new plants can grow. Seeds come in all sorts of shapes and sizes and they have all kinds of crazy ways to try to get to a new place to grow. This is called dispersal. Why not go on a seed hunt to find seeds that are dispersed in different ways?

You will need:

A fine day in late summer or fall (autumn)

Some egg cartons with lids

A backpack to carry them in

1 On a fine day in late summer or fall (autumn), set off on your seed hunt with your egg cartons in a backpack so that your hands are free. Your seed hunt could be around your backyard or you could ask an adult to take you to woods, fields, or a park. Everywhere you go you will find seeds of all shapes and sizes inside seed cases of all shapes and sizes. Try to collect different types in the compartments of your egg cartons. Keep the cartons upright in your pack!

SAFETY

Always wash your hands after you have been exploring outside.

2 Find seeds like dandelions, with feather-light parachutes. These are blown around by the wind. Blow some from a plant and see how far they go.

3 Find a winged seed with a helicopter action—sycamore or maple trees have these. As they fall from the trees they spin. This means they take longer to fall and so the wind has more chance to catch them and whisk them to somewhere new. Stretch up high and drop a handful to see them spin.

Which SEEDS can FLY?

4 Find seeds that stick to your clothes or your dog's fur. Look at each one closely and you will see it is covered in tiny hooks. When you or an animal shakes one off it will fall in a different place.

5 Find a pepper pot! Poppy seeds come in "pepper pots." When they dry, their seed cases have tiny holes around the top. The wind blows, shaking the pot, and the tiny seeds are shaken out.

6 Find some nuts. Nuts have hard shells inside an outer covering, which can be quite thin like a hazelnut, or prickly like chestnuts. Squirrels love nuts and they bury them to eat in the winter but they often forget where they have put some of them. These can grow into new trees.

7 Find some blackberries and look for purple bird poo nearby. Birds love juicy berries but the seeds inside the berries go right through them and come out the other end. The seed starts to grow in its own little pile of manure.

8 Find some pine cones whose woody scales are open. Shake the seeds out. The scales only open when the seeds are ripe and then they can shake out in the wind. Some pine seeds have wings so they can blow farther in the wind.

9 Find some seeds that grow in pods like peas. When the pods dry they split open suddenly and the seeds shoot out.

10 You may be lucky and find some other exploding seed cases. You can hear these pop and the seeds might even hit you. They usually explode in the sun on hot days when their seed pods dry out or when you touch them.

11 What is the biggest seed you can find and what is the smallest?

The science
BEHIND THE MAGIC

To grow well, seeds need to find some good soil with enough water, light, and space around them. If they all just drop off their parent plant, they will all be trying to grow in one place—it will be too crowded and the parent plant will take all the nutrients. So the plant tries to disperse its seeds as widely as possible. Plants may produce thousands of seeds but only a very few land in the perfect spot and grow into a new plant.

Index

Useful websites
www.rokit.com (for water rocket kits)
www.miniscience.com (US online store for buzzers, wires, and battery holders)
www.tts-group.co.uk (US online store for buzzers, wires, and battery holders)

A note on molecules
Molecules are what everything is made of and every different material has a different size and shape of molecule. Molecules are so small that nobody can see them, except with an electron microscope. They are made of different types and numbers of atoms (which are even smaller particles) joined together in different patterns. For example, a water molecule (H_2O) is made up of two hydrogen atoms joined together with one oxygen atom.

The plastic you made on page 10 is a simple one called casein. When the milk reacts with the vinegar, the casein is left in blobs. Casein molecules are like long strings which are similar to the plastic molecules made from oil. As the casein dries it hardens because the molecules pull together more tightly.